WORLD OF COLORS

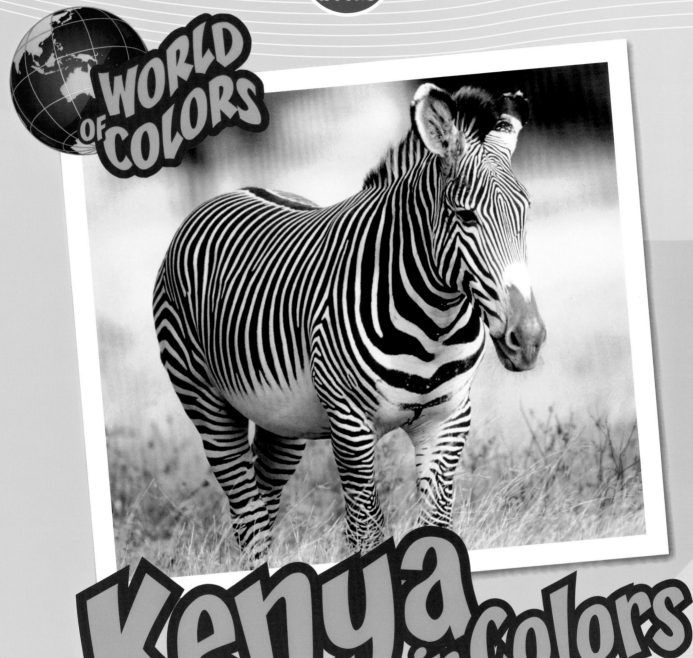

Kenya in Colors

by Sara Louise Kras

Consultant: David P. Sandgren
Professor of History
Concordia College
Moorhead, Minnesota

Capstone press

Mankato, Minnesota

Orange cheetahs live on the flat grasslands of Kenya. Cheetahs are the world's fastest land mammals. They can run up to 70 miles (113 kilometers) per hour.

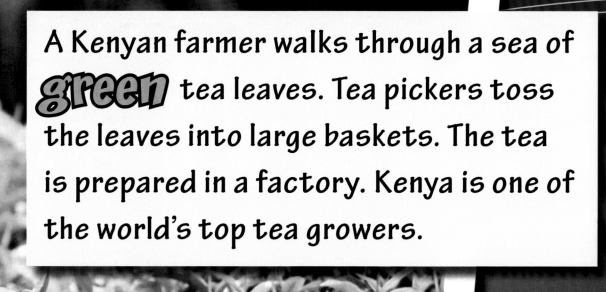

A Kenyan farmer walks through a sea of **green** tea leaves. Tea pickers toss the leaves into large baskets. The tea is prepared in a factory. Kenya is one of the world's top tea growers.

Young Maasai warriors wear **red** cotton robes while dancing. Both men and women wear colorful beaded necklaces. The Maasai live in southern Kenya. They raise cattle, sheep, and goats.

Elephants covered in **brown** dust lumber across a dirt road. Many of Kenya's animals are protected in national parks and reserves. Tourists from around the world visit these parks each year. They come to see elephants and other wild animals.

Kenyan students in **green** uniforms take a break from school to play outside. They study math, history, and geography. They are also taught two languages, English and Kiswahili.

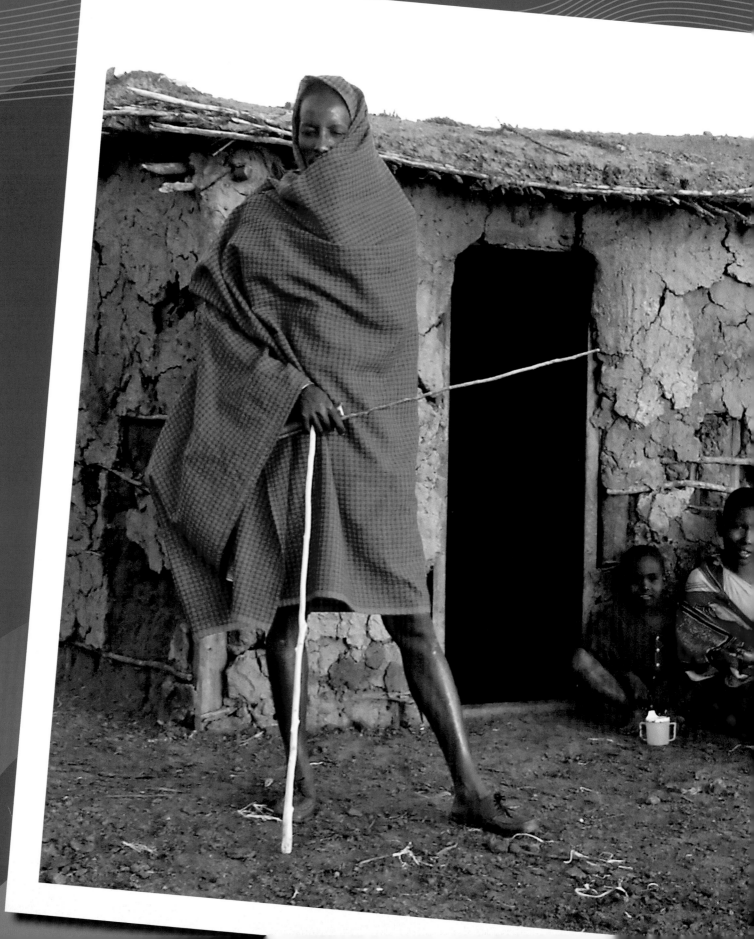

A Maasai man in a **purple** robe stands in front of his home. The Maasai build their homes with mud, cow dung, and sticks. The rooms inside are used for cooking and sleeping. At night, some farmers bring their animals inside to sleep.

Crispy **gold** samosas are a popular Kenyan snack. Samosas are made of fried pastry. They are stuffed with potatoes, peas, and meat. Many Kenyans buy samosas at outdoor food stands.

A **gray** statue of Jomo Kenyatta sits against the **blue** sky in Nairobi. Jomo Kenyatta helped Kenya become a country. He was also the first Kenyan president.

Kenyan farm workers carry **red** and **green** coffee berries in **brown** buckets. Coffee is an important crop for Kenya. It is sold to countries around the world.

White buildings line a quiet street in Mombasa. Mombasa is Kenya's most important port on the Indian Ocean. Ships carry goods from Mombasa to other countries. Mombasa also has its own airport and many hotels.

A **brown** volcano sits in Lake Turkana. Human and animal fossils have been found on its shores. Some of these fossils are millions of years old.

Young Kenyan scouts in *yellow* scarves march in a Madaraka Day parade. Madaraka Day is an important national holiday in Kenya. It celebrates Kenya's first independent government.

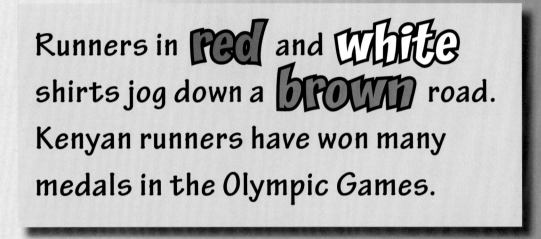

Runners in **red** and **white** shirts jog down a **brown** road. Kenyan runners have won many medals in the Olympic Games.

FACTS about Kenya

Capital City: Nairobi

Population: 37,953,838

Official Languages: English and Kiswahili

Common Phrases

English	Kiswahili	Pronunciation
hello	jambo	(JAHM-bo)
good-bye	kwaheri	(kwuh-HAIR-ee)
yes	ndio	(en-DEE-oh)
no	hapana	(hah-PAH-nah)

Map

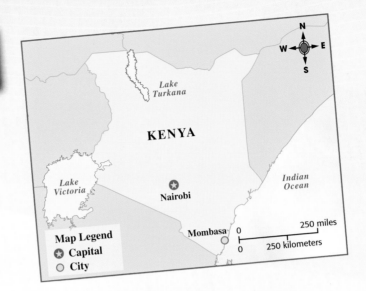

Flag

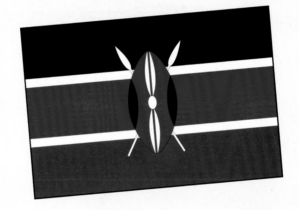

Money

Kenyan money is called the Kenyan shilling. One shilling equals 100 cents.

Glossary

dung (DUHNG) — solid waste from animals; the Maasai use cow dung to build their homes.

fossil (FOSS-uhl) — the remains or traces of an animal or a plant, preserved as rock

grassland (GRASS-land) — a large, open area where grass and low plants grow

lumber (LUHM-bur) — to move at a slow pace

Maasai (MAH-sigh) — an ethnic group of people in Kenya who raise cattle, sheep, and goats for a living

mammal (MAM-uhl) — a warm-blooded animal with a backbone; female mammals feed milk to their young.

Olympic Games (oh-LIM-pik GAMES) — sports contests among athletes from many nations

port (PORT) — a harbor where ships dock safely

reserve (ree-ZURV) — a place set aside for animals to live

volcano (vol-KAY-noh) — a mountain with vents; lava, ash, and gas erupt out of the vents.

Read More

Haskins, Jim, and Kathleen Benson. *Count Your Way through Kenya.* Count Your Way. Minneapolis: Millbrook Press, 2007.

Thompson, Lisa. *Amazing Africa.* Read-it! Chapter Books. SWAT. Minneapolis: Picture Window Books, 2006.

Internet Sites

FactHound offers a safe, fun way to find Internet sites related to this book. All of the sites on FactHound have been researched by our staff.

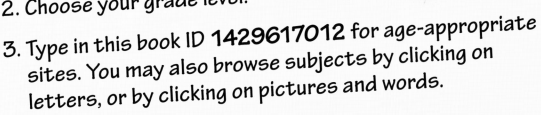

Here's how:

1. Visit www.facthound.com

2. Choose your grade level.

3. Type in this book ID **1429617012** for age-appropriate sites. You may also browse subjects by clicking on letters, or by clicking on pictures and words.

4. Click on the **Fetch It** button.

FactHound will fetch the best sites for you!

Index

A+ Books are published by Capstone Press,
151 Good Counsel Drive, P.O. Box 669, Mankato, Minnesota 56002.
www.capstonepress.com

1 2 3 4 5 6 13 12 11 10 09 08

Library of Congress Cataloging-in-Publication Data
Kras, Sara Louise.
　Kenya in colors / by Sara Louise Kras.
　　p. cm. — (A+ books. World of colors)
　　Summary: "Simple text and striking photographs present Kenya, its culture,
and its geography" — Provided by publisher.
　　Includes bibliographical references and index.
　　ISBN-13: 978-1-4296-1701-7 (hardcover)
　　ISBN-10: 1-4296-1701-2 (hardcover)
　　1. Kenya — Juvenile literature. 2. Kenya — Pictorial works — Juvenile literature.
　I. Title. II. Series.
DT433.522.K73 2009
967.62 — dc22
　　　　　　　　　　　　　　　　　　　　　　　　　　　　　　　2008005274

Credits
Megan Peterson, editor; Veronica Bianchini, designer; Wanda Winch, photo researcher

Photo Credits
Alamy/Images of Africa Photobank/Frank Nowikoski, 10–11; AP Images/Sayyid Azim,
25; Art Life Images/age fotostock/Ken Welsh, 20–21; Art Life Images/Gavriel Jecan,
cover; Getty Images Inc./John Gichigi, 27; Getty Images Inc./Reportage/Christopher
Pillitz, 18–19; Getty Images Inc./Stone/Mitch Kezar, 8–9; Getty Images Inc./Stone/Paul
Kenward, 4–5; James P. Rowan, 6–7; Nature Picture Library/Richard Du Toit, 22–23;
Paul Baker, 29 (coins); Peter Arnold/Oldrich Karasek, 17; Photos.com, 1, 2 (cheetah
running); Shutterstock/Andrew Chin, 29 (flag); Shutterstock/Birute Vijeikiene, 12–13;
Shutterstock/Colin & Linda McKie, 14–15; Shutterstock/Mityukhin Oleg Petrovich, 29
(banknote); Shutterstock/Roman Kobzarev, 2–3 (cheetah face)

Note to Parents, Teachers, and Librarians
This World of Colors book uses full-color photographs and a nonfiction format
to introduce children to basic topics in the study of countries. *Kenya in Colors*
is designed to be read aloud to a pre-reader or to be read independently by an
early reader. Photographs help listeners and early readers understand the text
and concepts discussed. The book encourages further learning by including the
following sections: Facts about Kenya, Glossary, Read More, Internet Sites, and
Index. Early readers may need assistance using these features.